The Essential Space of Play

Also by George Genovese and published by Ginninderra Press
Time Steals Softer
Love Letters to the World

George Genovese

The Essential Space of Play

The Essential Space of Play
ISBN 978 1 74027 759 4
Copyright © text George Genovese 2012
Cover painting *Boy* by Jason Beale,
photographed by Marek Witkowski

First published 2012
Reprinted 2017

Ginninderra Press
PO Box 3461 Port Adelaide 5015
www.ginninderrapress.com.au

Contents

Clown	7
Bureaucrat	8
Air	10
War Parade	11
Silence	12
Time Steals Softer (II)	13
The Curio Shop and the Faded Gleam	14
Flight of the Crow	15
Regret	16
Stabbing	19
Ladybird	21
My Face	22
Mirror	25
Listless Night	26
Playing Marbles at Recess	27
Salvation	28
Archaic Footprints	29
Musician	31
Time	32
Sparrow on a Kiosk	33
Augur of Approaching Rain	35
The Forgotten Moment Before Writing	36
Conscious	38
Ease	39
Faith	40
Supermarket	41
Somewhere	43
Towards a Common Truth	44
Patriots	45
Baudelaire	47

Verlaine	48
Mallarmé	49
Nocturne – a Lullaby	50
A Community of Tree	51
The Passing Poem	53
Commerce	56
Ennui	57
Silke	58
TV Moment	59
The Condemned Tick	60
Childhood	61
Harlot	62
Prayer	63
Drought	64
The Gift – Friendship	65
Solitude	66
Hold Hope	67
The Figment	68
Peace	70
The Essential Space of Play	72
Lament	73

Clown

See how his art
belies itself,
how clumsiness
is consummate skill
and years of practice.

Observe the way
he plays intent
against its end,
attains success
in seeming failure,
transforms a tent

into a space
of universal
absurdity
or cosmic malice,
a recalcitrant
reality

of human frailty
and fraught endeavour;
how wonderfully
subversive is
his play of wild

imagination,
that easy seems
the difficult
and serious work
of laughter.

Bureaucrat

His words precise,
allowing him
their loopholes –
your appeals are vain.

Grudgingly
beholden to
a memory
of justice, careful
of litigation,
he keeps his language
technically terse.
These days, where truth
has no inherent
meaning, depend
on juggled words.

Decorous, bland,
self-servingly vague,
suggestive of
a fugitive hope
you find – you're trapped!

His look concerned,
your plight, alas,
does not accord
with his demands.
His pleasantries,
soothingly polite,
perfunctory,
he makes you feel
you somehow owe
him gratitude
for his so delicate
and civil cant;

skilful, unctuous,
his language like
a warm secretion
oozing in
a pleasant film
inside his pants,
he sits there smiling,
uncomprehending,
while yet, *again*,
you try to make
your suffering plain.

Air

If air could rest
upon itself,
a tangible thing
as leaf upon
a leaf, then I
would have a book
of poems.

War Parade

It's sadly strange
that we must first
display hostility
before a cooler mind
and calmer head
seek peace instead.

And tragic too
that many souls
must first be lost
before the common pain
of sacrifice
thinks on the price.

First thought as other,
your foe, like you,
grieves for his brother,
asks why it took his death
for he and you
to march together;

why you and he
were bent on rage
and hate gone rife
before a torn human
ity affirmed
not war, but life?

Silence

For fear of facing an uneasy silence
we spear the air with words, betray our violence
through prematurely bearing mangled language,
our thought disfigured to a stillborn sound.
A brutal moment must be deftly bandaged,
the septicaemic soul re-dressed and bound,
for silence brings before our inner eyes
those toxic truths that haunt unwholesome lives:
our constant chatter merely masks our lust
and feigned concern our false humility,
our show of care a snare for those who trust
and friendly words good form's sterility –
ten times today we've wished each other dead
but babbled on about the weather instead…

Time Steals Softer (II)

for Lawrence Whiffin

Time steals softer than the light,
spreads beyond a nascent vision
scanning open sky; unfolding
past horizons of an arching
depth and height, time slinking slyly
binds a seeing to its site…

Time glides softer than a glance,
orbits with a gentler motion
than a pining gaze; suspending
objects in the spectral lightness
of its press, it passes frailer
than the shyest eye's caress.

Time falls softer than the night,
tapers to a dusky velvet's
calm unruffled quiet; fainter
than a trace of breath dispersing
out of sight, it narrows to a
darkness clipped of vision's flight.

The Curio Shop and the Faded Gleam

A motley throng of figurines contend
for space upon a shelf. Old wizards, knights
and pirates jostle Jesus and his saints.
How soulless seems the semblance they intend,
these buccaneers and men of holy heights
of moulded plastic garbed in gaudy paint.
When still a child their brilliance would have drawn
me in a dream of dazzled wonder, borne
me to a world of unsurpassed adventure
where armour gleamed and painted faces breathed;
back then they shone with a light my eyes could see
and as I puzzle how I gleaned such splendour,
I see no radiant thing or toy unsheathed
that gleam, but mirrored back that glow from me.

Flight of the Crow

Disturbed at vision's margin by a soft
commotion, swift surprise directs me to
a leaf-cloaked crow alighting on a tree.
With faintly flashing claps of wings awaft,
it fails to settle from my partial view,
attempting its descent unceasingly…
I try to glean what keeps this struggling crow
from perching in quiescence on its bough
and, drawing near, discover no such bird,
but just a sable strip of flapping plastic.
Before this artefact I stop and stare,
think on that crow distinctly seen and heard,
convinced that past this flapping motion, spastic,
that swift departed crow still wings somewhere.

Regret

Alone before the mirror, head in hand,
and staring blankly at herself, her eyes
survey the grey and muddy vestiges of
her once resplendent raven hair. She turns
her head and with a sidelong glance regards
a crow's foot at the corner of an eye.
Peevishly distorting her appearance,
she grimaces to see if she can still
adopt a winning or alluring smile.
'There's still attractiveness and charm,' she thinks,
but then those sallow teeth offend with age.
With an abrupt and almost mechanical
reflex she ceases smiling, crimps her brow,
and barely audibly, quite unaware
she does so, sighs. A moment later she
becomes aware of the musty smell of dust
her inadvertent exhalation stirred…

As if the glass reflected back her past,
she sees her one true chance at love before
her. There he stands in all his youthful pride!
There they are, both disporting on the grass,
rejoicing like two children at mock fights,
too innocently seeking an excuse
to touch each other. For he loved her as she
loved him, yet both lacked courage to provoke
the moment to the crisis of that first
and longed-for kiss. It always seemed to her
their union would inevitably happen,
she hesitated out of modesty,
a native shyness which she shared with him
and not for lack of love or secret doubt,

rather, intensity of love which held
her back – the fact she held him in such awe…

So she deferred decision, he did too,
succumbing to the youthful illusion that
they both possessed an infinite time! She should
have been more brave, more bold, and let him know
she was his rightful claim, let herself go,
and on one of their many nightly walks
pretended she was cold, implied a way,
to make it known this was her invitation
for him to sidle up and keep her warm,
but they just talked, and talked…and talked. And she
continued waiting, wondering, hesitating,
always mistaking tomorrow for her hope…

II

The day he suddenly introduced her to
his lover, ambushed in complete surprise,
she froze in silence, feigning an outward poise
while inwardly reeling to that sudden shock;
beneath her calm demeanour and self-control,
she felt her world, each tender dream and sweet
sustaining hope come crashing down around
her in a harsh and catastrophic stroke!

It seemed her life had ended, but in time
convinced herself that she was strong enough
to cope, sincerely wished the man she loved
all happiness and sought to carry on,
to forget and spurn resentment or regret,

and just accept the growing distance that
had crept between them till they lost all touch.
And yet her waiting was still not done,
for somewhere, still sequestered in her heart
a seeding vestige of persistent love
sustained itself on dreams of his return.
Although she put all thoughts of him outside
her mind and wouldn't admit that this was so,
she still did nothing all those years to find
new love. Like someone frozen in the past,
a tender soul so overcome with loss
she saw no forward way beyond that loss,
and made a vocation of her pent-up grief…
Though fruitless waiting had become the snare
by which she found herself alone, she knew
no other way and made that snare her home…

Today an old acquaintance called her up
to tell her he had died two days ago.
'His last reflections, as his heart,' she said,
'remained with you. He'd had a happy life,
fulfilled in every way, a loving wife
and children, but had never altered in
his love for you. "My shyness was my curse,"
he said. "I never dared to dream that one
as beautiful as her could feel for me
a commensurate esteem. If only she
had felt the same, I'd part the world
without resistance for that one regret.
Please tell her I love her and always did."'

Stabbing

From years of huddled hurt
and cornered fear, immured
from human height in a downcast
camouflage of silence,

his holed up, darting eyes,
tormented cat-toyed mice,
uneasily shifting in
the hemmed-in squalor of

their darkness, he, at last,
with hair-spring trigger hand
retracted, tautly wound
to snapping point, released

its thrust of blade to feel
a punctured heart explode
beneath its plunge…
From years of suffered taunts

and stifled screams, he heard
another's tearing skin
and fearful cry as if
it were his victor's song;

set at a safe remove
and distance from himself,
the gouging plough of pain
and past refraining moan

unbound, arose and voiced
a triumph over all
his exiled days and nights.
But then the wide-eyed stare,

the dying flutter, pall
and grip of blood that warmed
his hand. The sudden sane
voice from the madness of

his rage with its 'My god
what have I done!' The terror,
panic, flight – and all
his troubles just begun…

Ladybird

Over a pitching reach of intersecting
ripples and through a flux of seething bubbles,
a struggling ladybird wends the backyard channels.
Past shipwrecked bottle tops and foundering
twigs, between the mammoth hulks of listed
snails, she winds a tremulous course around
the pot plant citadels looming in a spray
of mist. Steady-as-she-goes through clumps
of mangroves in the cracks, she threads
a way into the driveway's open main,
where, pounded by rain and whirled by wind,
she runs a-ground on the final island to the drain.
Becalmed inside the shifting eye of the storm,
one mighty buffet might still dislodge her
from her precarious berth, precipitate
her down the roaring cataract with all
the day's debris. There, lashed and tossed on her
submerging haven, furiously fighting
the pull of the drain's Leviathan jaw
whose groaning darkness fans her anguished face,
she laments that her heroic journey of
an epic eighty feet should come to this.

My Face

And when all's said and done
won't everyone see past
this face? It's graven lines
of age, the gashes through
which sealed-up darkness seeps?
Each sallow crimp and fold,
a history told of all
it's sensual fury, hot
pursuit of lust and hate,
its searing anger for
the pain it couldn't efface,
the rippling envy written
for another's better fate
retraced in every telltale
line and frowning crease…

And God its vanity,
its prizing of itself
as if it clung to something
more than just a nest
of worms, its puffed-up pride
and bluster, appetite
for its own flattery
and self-important storms;
its craven core when it
cast off the harder task
of generosity
and spurned the burden of
a sacrifice before
the poorer hearts it crossed!

And when all's said and done,
this face of broken clouds
and puff of smoke dispersing
in an empty space devoid
of a warming sun, revealed
a vast vacuity
of soul in the phantom
image of slavery
it mastered as its own;
these furtive eyes that stalked
in orbits fraught with terror,
and in the circuits of
their turning forged the chains
of error in which vision
snagged and caught. The eloquent
voice whose high-flown rhetoric
proved to be no more
than tongue-tied talk, its fealty
bought and sold when courage,
help and hope were needed most.

What good is age if still
a lifetime's lead of baseness
never once transformed
or even strove for that
alchemic change into
a soulful gram of gold?

But one thing left for that
which thought of naught and told
of nothing past itself –
I hear it sounding in
the nearing thunder of
a hammer's fall – I hear
it in the final script
of flaking skin and flying
shards of chiselled bone.
The last inscription hammered
on a face's last blank space
towards its grave-ward jaw
will be the epitaph
which tells that face it lived
and died, but still remained unborn.

Mirror

Like a fleeting breeze wafting over a lake,
sometimes the Spirit passes…
One pauses, feels the lightness of its tread,
and trembles at its presence.
Though its gentle press stirs the feeblest ripples,
an inner tremor cuts the deep…

And when it's passed, one stands transfixed
with searching eyes intent
on inward distances opened in its wake.
One follows into silence
the vastness of a landscape spread
before a wondering gaze;

then the soul grown steady in contemplation,
its face a spotless mirror,
retrieves a pristine order settled to
unruffled peace, and earth
and sky drawn near and clear, stand in
the stillness of its face…

Listless Night

In the still nocturnal hours of sleeplessness,
time dragging like a fishnet scraped across
your brain, you lay half wakeful in the murk
and hear that dredging fishnet creak with stress;
a tangled mass of thoughts and images toss
amid the strain of winches at their work,
emerge from clanking mind's machinery
as it hauls strange monstrosities from the deep.
Bizarre aquatic creatures flap and float
before the closed eyes' unrelenting vision,
disjointed thoughts in ceaseless, vague refrains
struggle to link the sense which slips their grope –
as if these scenes of tedious repetition
implied an overlooked imploring, 'Change!'

Playing Marbles at Recess

It must have been a strangely marvellous moment,
so gathered in itself that just a game
of marbles could exist, a game, ourselves,
and the immediate earth beneath our feet
or knees. Wrapped in a concentration only
children absorbed in playing can command,
both striving for our very best, the wide
world vanished to a blissful point of focus.

But then we felt the guilty silence stare
at us, and looking up in disbelief,
so saw the playground filled with screaming kids
a moment ago suddenly deserted.
'How could we have missed the bell?' we wondered
'Not heard those children disappearing with
their noisy ebb?' Wrenched from our place of play
and its consuming peace, we found ourselves
again within objective time and space,
there spread before us as an empty ground…

It must have been a strangely marvellous moment,
but like such moments, lost as soon as found,
or if not lost entirely, captured as
a fleeting memory outside itself…
So back in time, but with no time to waste,
we scooped our marbles up and scurried back
towards the adult world we'd left behind,
that place of sums and tests where someone wore
a peevish frown and held a rod in hand,
the threat of punishment always in our face.

Salvation

Who is the enemy of man –
the godless who destroys a cherished dream,
or else the keeper of a needful lie?
And where a common silence waits
each teller of his side, then does
it matter in the end?

Who is the nurturer of man –
the truthful man with horror as his prize,
or the believer who engenders hope?
And where a hope and truth contend
and are to each an alien dark,
who triumphs in the end?

Archaic Footprints

(Going to work)

I must confess, the way she fluidly entered
the tram with a swivel of her narrow hips,
a lunging gait and twist, provoked the vision
of a simian woman with a baboony rump.
And when, with chimp-like ears, she drew and gazed
into a portable mirror, pursed her lips
and smeared her lipstick with aplomb, again,
I couldn't escape the image of a pretty monkey
at its game of putting its human mask on.

Beside the tram in rows of banked-up cars
was more of the same; almost as if I were
aloft in some tall tree, I watched them there
below, distracted as they waited for the lights
to turn: the ruminating man who chewed
his gum as if it were a luscious banana
or leaf; the preening woman, flicking her fringe,
checking for split-ends as though she'd suddenly
entrapped another louse to crush between
her teeth; the children, playfully pummelling, tumbling
from the imagined branches of a car's back seat,
digesting gleefully in their Jaguar's belly...

There, rows and rows of caged orangutans
dreamt solemnly of better times, their brains
bedazzled by a teeming forest of signs,
or, sheltered in their coverts of technology,
bizarre, sophisticated primates tapped
impatient opposable thumbs on what was just
a Pliocene age ago (an eye's mere blinking)
no wheel for steering but the latest flint
for the cracking open of recalcitrant nuts.

The Alpha Romeo male, impatient to lead
the pack anticipates the changing lights
and then he's off – a plume of burning tires
and choking smoke in his exuberant wake,
and then the carbon pall the others fart
as they advance spreads like a curtain of
primeval mist to which the world reverts…

Some days it's just like this, this human show
and unaccountable drama, somewhat surreal,
and more than a little grotesque, and seems
to suggest that in two hundred millennia
a clever primate's scarcely learnt more than
to smear a violent footprint on its time,
to toss his excrement not just to earth,
but with blithe triumph, even to the sky!

Musician

(for Mario Genovese)

My mandolin, there's such a purity
of sweetest sound you render through each string,
and lovely too your body on the eye;
in truth, your soulful sound and perfect form
must be in mutual accord, as one,
for you to yield up just this honest tone…

With your round shoulder and its inward curve
so rolling to a flaring hip and rump,
how like a beautiful woman's shape you are;
if only you could be that tender one
who'd lie relaxed upon my lap while I
caressed her neck, to draw with gentle skill

her happy sighs and rising moans of pleasure,
or share with her the bitter lay of our
mortality, that through the harmony
of our well-tempered selves of flesh and blood
a striving art might gain its guiding goal
and very heart and soul of music – love.

Time

A smudge am I,
a trace,
in time
this photograph
will be all
remembered of
my face.

More tenuous yet,
a scent,
photos crumble
epitaphs wear,
none will know
I came –
and went.

Sparrow on a Kiosk

A sparrow's clear
and cheery
chirrup,

no tabloid tongue
and grisly
gossip

of who dumped whom:
the wooed
and won

and cuckold of
a loose
cuckoo.

A mellow sweet
and pure
musician,

no juggled word
of
politician

but straight-out song
and truthful
twitter,

which is to say,
no liar-
bird

or semantic
beautician's
chitter,

which is to say
a warbled
patter

that will not fib
or falsely
flatter.

Now hear her pitch
and sober
strain?

No bribe for me –
tomorrow
rain.

Augur of Approaching Rain

Those swallow-circling eyes that dart
about so grieve my doubting heart;
weaving around a question, their flight
averting mine, they flee the heights
and flutter softly near the ground.
Wavering, stealthy, without a sound,
they hint our summer's over-ripe
and weeping fruit is all we'll reap…
To you whose swerving look might ask,
'How doubt the sunshine where we bask?'
I'd say, 'Those swallows, swooping low,
those sweeping swallows say it's so.'

The Forgotten Moment Before Writing

It is the poem I never write I know
will vex me to my death,
that one I leave because it comes
as if unrealised, clumsy and pre-lingual,
and which demands the greatest work.
Lisping and stuttering, its palate cleft,
a badly literate waif,
I have much advice for her, this poem,
yes much, except for care…
She, to whom I say then, 'Go away
and come back poised and studied,
accomplished with an elocutionary grace!'

And yet it is you, sweet child,
most beautiful, most honest in
your earnestness I never understood,
your immediate 'Stop and look
and hear my faulty music run
inside your head!'
You were the one who simply thought
the kissing tongue to ear
demanded nothing but truth's word.
'All deft enunciation,
all craft depends on this,' you said.

You went away unheard and disappointed.
As I looked after you with my bewildered gaze,
a rag still in my hand with which I'd buff
a burnished monument, something about
you made me stare and wonder, something I'd
not noticed and, as usual, left unsaid…

And then it came – you came. The moment, *now*,
your truth, it came! You see I realised!
You were the poem I live but cannot write,
the visitation, frightening and friendly,
at once accomplished, broken and familiar, yet
still surprising, baffling, despite your easy and
as-if-we-knew-each-other-from-eternity manner;
you see, I saw, at last, you came to say,
(quite reasonably, I think)
'I am that simplest of children, wise and ancient,
here to haunt you to your end!'

Conscious

You are the elemental mystery,
an intricate creation,
that blend of earth and water, fire and air,
yet more than just their combination.

You come as one and yet a pair,
the contradiction's necessary Other,
the light and dark whose sense
is found in that which gathers them together.

The site of truth and axis of perception,
the height and depth of soul, immense,
yet lover of all ways to self-evasion
throughout perception's trance.

You paradox and puzzle,
what is this thing and point of pivotal strength?
This thing that's shifting in its stance
and gliding to its permanence in death?

Not beast nor angel but the melded twain,
an untapped godhead's wealth,
the self-creating quest to that called 'man'
and question turning on itself.

Ease

Just like a steadfast tree to which a gaze
sedately faces – noting casually
its mighty trunk and then the well-placed boughs
alternately arranged upon its axis,
and then from these in lateral array
its branches, then again its stalks and twigs;
and then, beguiled through every visual turn,
extended, the final echoed limit of its leaves
completes this radiant movement and expansion,
that from the constant play of forms, unique,
the asymmetry of each particular and
meandering line and vagrant rhythm, each
resplendent curve, a sudden harmony
emerges as the total vision of the tree;
and where, just now, seen through its airy bulk,
the seeping angles of the sky beyond
appear as consonantal fragments of
a natural mosaic, a realised perfection
of some fortuitously found design
that can't but tranquillise the restively
distracted eye and mind – such is my mood,
delighting in the order of its ease.

Faith

I tried to hold the running world
as it went hurtling in a flood,
but then my fist became a heart
and water turned to running blood.

I tried to seize it in the craft
that told me art can conquer time,
but when I opened up my hand
I only found accruing grime.

So then I drew my love to me
and told her softly with a kiss –
'Whatever else may spell defeat,
I shall, with you, succeed in this!'

And so I held her close to me
and kept my faith with every breath,
and knew I'd won at least in life
what yet might be destroyed in death.

Supermarket

There, shimmering by the parking lot,
out of the sun's barrage,
the supermarket rises up –
an oasis or mirage?

So in you drive your searing car,
and find a place to park it,
then cross the hot Sahara tar
to reach the supermarket.

Amid the air-conditioned breeze
and soothing, soft muzak,
you're like a camel now relieved
from the luggage on its back;

or there beside the mineral springs,
a Schweppes being your intent,
you feel you've been invited in
a sultan's lavish tent.

The wealth of all Arabia
awaits each sultan's whim,
indeed the bounty of the world
in plastic, box or tin.

Here every wish is satisfied,
no velleity too small,
and lovely check-out harem girls
give their submissive all.

Ten thousand times you'll hear them sing
with voices low and sweet
when asking, 'How are you?'
to the bar code's tuneful beep!

Abreast of you a woman scolds
her children's sweet-toothed whims,
and just now she a merchant seems
beset by Bedouins.

But now it's time to face the heat
and leave the breezy store,
to give your bag up to the gaze
of the eunuch by the door.

Somewhere

Somewhere there are rolling hills
and azure skies and plains,
where meaning runs in crystal streams
and not down human drains.

Somewhere there are verdant lands
by tender winds caressed,
and, unlike here, the sky meets earth
like lovers gently pressed.

Somewhere past mere memory
a mind still heeds a heart
and man and beast are foremost – beings,
not digits on a chart.

Somewhere other than this place
of steel and asphalt hives,
communion and not commerce reigns
those otherworldly lives.

Yes, somewhere, blessed, horizons stretch
as far as eyes can span,
and truth and beauty still transcend
the fallow wastes of man.

Towards a Common Truth

And if I set a golden truth in words
to guide you through your years
would you listen any harder
than if I'd written it in tears?

You look to a space of idealisation
where you can safely traffic,
well and good, my friend, I know the weight
of all your wordless panic.

We share the same unspoken pain
and couch it in the abstract 'man',
but it's the terror before each other
that wrings from each – I am.

Patriots

So these the patriots who send a nation's youth
to die in far-off lands,
who talk of truth and sanctity of life,
a thousand more abstractions dusted off
when need demands.

So these the patriots who rip their country's guts
for oil or mineral wealth,
who ravage her with naked savagery
and sully her with poisons for their profit
with venal stealth.

So these the patriots whose love was never more
than what they'd hoard or gain,
a narcissistic shibboleth whose worship
arrogates another's rightful share
with glib disdain.

O brothers who still struggle in your poverty,
good sisters who still cry
among the patriots who declaim their love,
there, cold beneath your flags and emblems, you
still hunger – why?

Poor fodder marching to an idiot-drum
of fated sacrifice,
it's you who forge your fates and woes to come,
why lend yourselves to madmen's lies when you
must pay their price?

Hunger for justice shan't be sated on
a self-exalting pride,
a truer love surpassing boundaries knows
the tribal mind must yield its first allegiance
to all mankind!

Baudelaire

As wisps of smoke insinuating through
the air, a blended fragrance for the few,
at once of ambergris and opiate plumes
pervading sumptuous rooms or whorehouse hovels,
of noxious wormwood and exotic perfumes
where man stands proud, or broken Spirit grovels,
reclaims composure in the moonlight quiet
or falls to drunken fits of blasphemous riot,
his music rises with seductive grandeur
and wafting over a soul mired in ennui,
meanders, lithe, like cobras of glowing amber
to spit its venom at its enemy.
Let all hell's horrors come for these he'll bless
as long this foe is conquered – Nothingness.

Verlaine

If sparsest music can disclose a space
made of diaphanous mist, then such a place
is this Parisian Park of muted tints
and opalescent air; such is this spare
suggested line of trees with prismal hints
of hue refracted through the rain they bear.
Where sensual music sculpts its nymphs and fawns
and spreads its bourgeois order, tidy lawns
belie the anguish of the unkempt soul,
its guilty hour of infidelities
and badly mannered truths… Leaves softly roll
upon a pool where searching eyes might seize
a faithful face – (reflections ripple, stir,)
the remade self beyond the present blur.

Mallarmé

White phantom on a plain of white – a ground
of silence where you rise in faintest sound,
are you a mirrored swan in icy snow
or, foam engulfed, a listing ship of froth?
Soft winter sky with a pallid cloud's dull glow,
or vase of crystal on its land of cloth,
you strain to be all these, yet none and more…
Amphora of all gathered metaphor,
and vessel for a spectral song, the space
where form and fluxing image coalesce
in quest to site their source, but only face
the ghostly void in which they effervesce –
from your white silence apparitions float
to fold before the Absence they connote.

Nocturne – a Lullaby

Sleep and be at peace
and greet relief
upon you stealing,
now have no haste
to be awake
and lose this balm of healing.

Forsake the world and let
it take its hours
of fretful weaving,
repose in peace
for soon, too brief,
you'll wake again to grieving.

A Community of Tree

We did not see when we
were gathered there together
that we were one community.

In radiant arrangement on
our branches, thrilled by the wind,
we did not see the sound we made

ascended as the rustles
of our harmonic tongues,
for such were we, each leaf a mouth,

but not the central voice
that could possess the song
whose only source remained the Tree.

And it was fine, so fine,
suspended there together,
sometimes sharing, sometimes competing

for a sprinkle of rain or shower
of sun, the while convinced
we did it by and for ourselves…

It mattered little then
to each sole leaf when one
should dry and die and fall to silence,

nor that a neighbour should
turn sickly with corruption
and slowly wither in our midst…

For then, I was this leaf
and you were that. And so,
in mutual dependence, blind that we

were one community,
corruption slowly spread
till *this* and *that* were both diseased.

In time, devoured by blight,
all leaves, limbs, crown and root,
fell victim to the same cruel fate.

***

No leaf am I and so,
before this withered Tree,
I stand as witness to this story.

One day I, who also
endure this malady
in an analogous fashion, may,

along with you, succumb
to the same pernicious poison.
Then, not even stories will be told.

The Passing Poem

To look at his burly body pressed
in tightly underneath his suit,
his thickset truckie girth
and powerful bricklayer arms
probably full of faded tats,
to hear his raw, cracked voice,
full of emotion, feminine in honesty,
in place of his native bellow
and nicotine rasp,
you think of how a week ago
you couldn't imagine
someone like him
up there weeping and reading
a self-made poem.
Perhaps then he would have made
an acerbic jibe and distanced
himself from all that pansy stuff,
perhaps,
now there he is…

The poem of passing, knotted with emotion,
raw-edged and chipped, broken and staggering,
plain talking without pretence,
brings together the threads of sundered lives,
faces distress defencelessly, boldly,
tears in its eyes,

'Twin brothers, Love and Death,
I know too well,'
the poem repeats, without directly saying.
'From ancient times to this,
this tale of warring brothers, Abel and Cain,
has been my greatest theme.
I have told and retold of their
inevitable clash, and even hinted
of some purpose found therein;
mostly for that I always come,
to tell again of purpose where
a chaos of emotion and assaulted
meaning would topple for
its overwhelming pain;
to clear a way of access for the tongue
through absence to remembrance, from
disordered loss to song,
that Love and Death might reunite
and meaning keep unharmed;

call it Cain's apology to the brother he loves,
his ceaseless attempt at his redeeming song…'

That man up there, who could
be anyone of us, instinctively knows
the scope and substance of the poem,
its inherent reality.
In the realm of Love and Death
there's none can take its place
or pattern so well an attitude
to a bitter passing…
Here, at least, by this coffin,
it would be a fool who says
the poem lies…

No, that man, almost a child
who knows the poem before
he's ever written one,
and lets its irresistible purpose
unwind from within, knows
its force in Love and Death
because it speaks with truth.

'Love, Love, Love and Death…'

His limping verse breaks off, hesitates,
echoes his uneasy shift, sniffles
as it regains a shattered composure;
crippled, it peers through cracks in its
own body, faces again the abyss,
then hobbles along…beautifully.

Commerce

It is a burden, heavy,
to bear this thought –
all beauty has been bought.

And so with any
commodity:
opinion, earth and hope.

As titles smudged
are acres of sky
beneath an owner's grope,

each leaf and mote,
each day and night
held by proprietary right.

Just this in our exchange
none would now own –
depreciated Soul.

Ennui

Heavier than a heart of rock
whose weight weighs down its song,
heavier than a yoke of bitter mocks
borne through a heartless throng,
heavier than effrontery
that greets you with a curse,
heavier more than memory
that lays hope in a hearse

is this fool's hour of restlessness
and empty weight of nothingness.

Silke

Yours is the broad and toothy smile,
the open arms' embrace, immense,
a heart delivered without guile
that welcomes me without pretence.

Yours are the wide and sparkling eyes
that seem to say, 'You, hiding there,
my love surpasses all your wiles
and can't contend with my soft care!

We have, together, gone as one
throughout the graveyard of ideals,
have found ourselves as woman, man,
in all the frailty each reveals;

and through this we've both grown in strength,
the richer for each hard-earned truth,
how strange – each moment's failing length
just deepened what was shallow youth.

Self-doubting lover do not fret
you somehow fail and disappoint,
it's you, who are no image met,
my heart sits with, as one, conjoint.

No, please don't turn against yourself
and make of something lovely, vile,
I care not for your faults or stealth
nor seek to put that self on trial!

What could you do to alter love
and make me gasp with rueful breath?
I'd only weep in sorrow of
your final act of selfless death!'

TV Moment

Monstrous upheaval, wanton barbarity,
foundations tumbling to the cry of millions,
a clarion call to madness, slaughter,
and triumphant nullity;

delirium's rule of cruel disorder,
a loosed and looming tragedy,
heralded here between the making
and the taking of a cup of tea.

The Condemned Tick

(Germany 2003)

'Is it my fault that I was born
offensive to your sight,
that I was made this humble form –
a tick and parasite,

while you a man, most fortunate,
who tower up so fair,
and truly, as I contemplate,
with so much blood to spare?

Why slander me, to you so strange,
who did not choose my feature,
and surely would, if I could change,
be made some fairer creature?'

'You speak the truth you bloated tick,
I too think life a sham,
for I would in a moment quick
be something more than man.

Alas, my nature's not so rare
as seems my outward guise,
but in its depth of fear, unfair,
decreed by One all-wise!

You see I anger quick to hate
and ruthlessly to damn –
for sure no God, I can't create,
but kill I surely can.'

Childhood

(Blue-remembered hills)

It was no fable Eden-land,
and I recall it still,
upon my way an angel flamed
and God each space did fill.

But then the exile swiftly came –
before I could have known,
my God and angel had withdrawn
and I to manhood grown.

Harlot

The harlot bears her body like a shopfront,
some of her choicest wares are on display –
only, one must first enter the doorway of
her mouth before one learns their cost.
In the windows of her soul a sign says, Open.

Prayer

That I could write the morning light which gilds
the dewy fields; that tinctured verses could
illume a page like sunshine laps a leaf;
that I could catch the dappled motion of
the sky-blue calm seen through the trembling trees,
and O! that words could eddy like the breeze.

That I could trace the interlacing lines
of purple shadows in the afternoon
and spread a friendly shade from which to view
a lucent day; great God, that I could use
a tuneful tongue to pay my time its due
and having spoken truly, truly lived!

Drought

(for Silke)

As if in a parched land devoid of pity,
a withered root entombed in dust
and wasted with tormenting thirst,
have I here waited in the broken earth.

As flowing water from a rock, as hope,
succour for one who languished in
the burning sun, so is the promise
of your return. Already I raise up

my wilted crown renewed in expectation
of when you'll soothe this barren sand,
already you, a welcome breeze,
approach me sweetly with the smell of rain.

The Gift – Friendship

Need to believe
to need
to go on,

aloneness would
declare
no need

to journey on,
but leave
me lost

before a step
had even
begun.

Need to be woven
where I
would be torn,

lovingly bowed
where I
would be frayed;

your strand my strand
in beauty
tied and shown,

and hopeful where,
alone,
I'd be afraid.

Solitude

In warm and joyous company
a soul indeed is blessed,
  but in the end
  all thoughts intend
a foot be homeward pressed.

When songs are sung, the din is done,
a weary soul craves rest,
  the more of spirit
  it did exhibit,
then solitude is best.

Hold Hope

It would be easy to give up – let go,
retire from struggle and admit defeat.
Hold hope, for none sees what tomorrow will show!

Don't say that 'Since the tears and time which flow
must only mean the sorrows that repeat,
it would be easy to give up – let go.'

Though phalanxes of anguish, row on row,
besiege you such surrender seems so sweet,
hold hope, for none sees what tomorrow will show!

Perhaps your triumph nears yet you don't know,
but for a doubtful outcome, still incomplete,
it would be easy to give up – let go.

What if for just another day or so
you botch the goal that was about replete?
Hold hope, for none sees what tomorrow will show!

Defy despair for that's your only foe,
affirm before that tyrant you'd unseat:
'It would be easy to give up – let go!
Hold hope, for none sees what tomorrow will show!'

The Figment

for Nathan Farrelly, who rightly pointed out I was one stanza short of a poem

There was an old figment who lived in a brain
and he had no features, no body or name;
no, he had no colour, no texture or shape,
nor walked with a patter, a tap or a scrape.

Not hairy or scaly, not feathered or furry,
the best one could say is he had to be blurry.
This poor little fella lacked even a scent,
not even a bloodhound could track where he went!

Though no one could say if he's fleshy or bony,
it's hard to conceive him as other than lonely.
So was he forsaken or sad or elated?
Alas, what he felt was never located,

for lacking a body that one could point out
the state of his feelings was somewhat in doubt
and since he was never demonstrably there
they came down to nothing, existing nowhere.

But surely there's nothing that comes out of nothing?
'Except for a figment!' this figment kept huffing.
'If only you knew my imaginary mother
you'd see that one figment can come from another!

Or were you acquainted with my Auntie Mirage,
her virtual offspring and fictions at large,
her vaporous husband, my Uncle Unreal,
you'd sense perhaps some things defy what you feel!

Yet though I might holler and rant and insist,
you'll blithely deny I ever exist…
I would be more forward if I had a choice,
my problem is this – I don't have a voice!

While some might call tragic this dubious state
I've come to accept my preposterous fate
and though I might vanish as soon as appear
it's really no matter for one who's not here!'

Peace

This, the quiet night
and space of respite
you overlook;
the narrow nook
through which a gaze,
pincered and grazed,
opens to view,
debouches through
the shattered shards
and clinging barbs
by which it bleeds
to take its ease.

And ah, at last,
outspread and cast
into the night,
beyond the sight
of bars begrimed
with rust and slime,
it rises, wafts
and draws its draught
and fill of stars;
from all that mars,
all fret and care,
ascending there…

Tomorrow's daze
returned, this gaze
then tearful, torn,
will come to mourn
the little lease
of parted peace
it briefly knew.
Then, toiling through
another hour
of drudgery dour,
know just this peace
by its decease.

The Essential Space of Play

(for Kris Hemensley)

These tedious blocks of monotone construction,
these uniform tracts of somnolent instruction
are like drab suburbs where one retires to die;
dour lines that lead like roads to bored conclusions
or grids of concrete ink, obscuring sky,
prosaic walls and fences of occlusion
proscribing where an eye might freely flow,
until, at last, amid each desolate row
of house and car, shop front and road, a glance
descries the clearing of an unkempt park!
There, where a child stands frozen in a trance,
a homemade kite describes a blissful arc,
and floating out, beyond the literal day,
glissades into the essential space of play.

Lament

Why sing
> you that song
>> to kingdom come?
> Why sing
>> you that sorrowing song?

> With a ting-a-ling-ling
> a harp and heart-string

> who is it
>> you woo the day long?

It is
> to the wind
>> and open air
> I sing
>> with sorrowing tear,

> a ting-a-ling-ling
> and broken heart string,

> for there is
>> no Other to hear.

www.ingramcontent.com/pod-product-compliance
Lightning Source LLC
Chambersburg PA
CBHW062153100526
44589CB00014B/1821